Exotic Gardening:
Learn To Grow
Tropical Fruits In
Non-Tropical Climate

JESSICA LIMA

TABLE OF CONTENT

Introduction

I would like to thank and congratulate you for downloading my book. I hope that you will enjoy reading this guide book on how to grow your own exotic fruits at home that will save you money and be chemical-free. You and your family can enjoy eating your own home-grown organic exotic fruits—just imagine the pride you will feel when you pick your own exotic fruits that you grew yourself!

You do not have to limit your fruit choice due to the area that you live. You can learn how to utilize the indoor spaces so that you are able to grow your own exotic fruits. I am sure that you are going to find this experience an exciting one that is going to offer you multiple benefits both financially and health wise.

In this book we will look at different kinds of fruits that you may grow, also look at the different environments you will need to create in order for your exotic fruit to flourish so that you can cultivate them. You will learn different tips and tricks that you can use in order to keep your inside garden healthy.

Chapter 1 – Exotic Tropical Trees You Can Grow Indoors

If you have a sun-room in your home that offers plenty of light with high ceilings, you can grow some tropical trees if you like. You must of course keep in mind how tall the trees are known to grow on average, some can grow as tall as twelve feet tall.

But if you have a home with high ceilings then this will not be much of a concern for you. You do want to offer the tropical trees lots of light, but we will talk about supplementing the light later in the book.

Below are a few tropical trees that you might consider growing:

- **Guava**—If you love the flavor or taste of guava fruit, you might consider growing a guava tree in your sun-room. Guava fruit is often expensive to by in the supermarkets, and it is usually seasonal as well, so it can be hard to get at times.

If you are a guava lover then it would be great for you to have your own guava tree that produces fruit for you all year round. The small white flowers of the guava tree release a lovely scent that will make your sun-room smell lovely.

When you first decide to plant your guava tree, and when you re-pot it, make sure that the soil you are using is rich with organic matter and is low in salt content otherwise your guava tree will not thrive. You will find that guava trees are pretty forgiving if you forget to water them, but they do like to be watered regularly. The guava tree prefers to be outside during the warm summer months, but remember to get your tree back inside before the frost comes.

Growing your own guava tree is a great way to bring some yummy tropical fruit into your home without added chemicals, or the expense of buying them in supermarkets. These trees are not a lot of work, you will pay initial expenses and then small expenses in keeping them healthy and you are all set to enjoy your homegrown guava fruit! What a lovely treat indeed to have your own fresh organic fruit that has been grown right under your own roof. I can assure you that you will enjoy this and benefit from it many times over.

- **Avocado**—If you are looking for a little challenge you can grow your own avocado tree right from an avocado seed, but this process will take a long time. It is very slim chances that you will actually get fruit. So if you want to get fruit your best bet would be to buy a plant from a nursery.

When it comes to avocado trees they are not keen on being over-watered and they prefer lots of natural sunlight. Take them outside during the summer months because they need the bees to pollinate them in order for them to produce fruit. But you must also remember to get them back indoors before the frost hits. To be on the safe side it is best that you only let your plants and trees stay outside during the hot summer months—as you don't want to risk exposing them to frost as this could lead to them dying off. Some plants are better at dealing with being exposed to frost than others. Many exotic plants do not deal well with frost exposure.

- **Papaya**—The papaya tree is quite similar to the banana tree. It is an attractive addition to any sun-room, but it is also large, and will have no trouble taking over a room if you allow it to. You can cut it back to keep the leaves and branches of it from getting out of control. This tree could easily reach the height of twelve feet or so. The papaya tree will grow rapidly and could within just a couple of years reach its mature height, The tree will not begin to actually produce fruit for another year or two after that.

- You need to have your papaya tree in an area that offers it lots of light as well as getting daily watering. It likes to have lots of humidity, just like a banana tree. If you do not have enough natural humidity, you can bring in a small humidifier and it will do the trick for you.

- **Banana**—Having your own banana tree will make a wonderful addition to your sun-room. The leaves on banana trees are massive and will produce a large amount of bananas as the plant matures and starts to produce fruit. It will take a few years for your banana tree to mature, but once it is mature you will get to enjoy the fruit from it all year round. You will also notice how much tastier your fruit from your tree tastes compared to store bought fruits. Think how fun it will be for your family members to go to the family banana tree and pick a fresh banana to add on top of their morning cereal or to take in their lunch for a snack at school. It will make a great conversation piece for anyone in your family to tell others that they are have their own banana tree in their house. I am sure people will be very amazed to see an indoor banana tree growing in your home.

Chapter 2 – Tropical Dwarf Trees

For those of us that do not have large amounts of space the dwarf trees are a great alternative. Dwarf trees are a great way to have a little bit of exotic in our home environment. Dwarf trees normally grow faster and produce fruit sooner than full-sized trees. Below are some dwarf trees that might interest you:

- **Dwarf Papaya Tree—**The dwarf variety of papaya trees grow to be about four feet tall, compared to the full-size tree that grow to around ten feet tall. The dwarf papaya prefers to be in full sunlight with moist soil, but not wet. It likes humidity, like most

other tropical fruit trees, so misting some water on the tree is a good idea, especially if you live in a dry area.

You can bring the feel of having tropical plants in your home with dwarf trees without having the feeling of your home being taken over like you might with a full-size tree. You can bring more of an assortment of dwarf trees into your sun-room area and you don't have to worry about them growing too big and tall.

- **Key Lime Tree**—You can have your key limes all year round because the key lime tree produces almost all year round. They have lovely small white flowers on them when they aren't producing limes that you can enjoy looking at as well as enjoy their lovely fragrance. This tree will reach about three feet tall. How nice this will be to have fresh limes all year round to add that special extra zip to your cooking flavors and drinks—your guests will love picking a fresh lime from your tree to add to their drinks.

Variegated Pineapple—This smaller version of the pineapple plant only reaches about a foot and a half. They will produce small pineapples that are still stunning to anyone that comes to visit. They are cream and red in color, which will draw people's attention to them. They also need plenty of sunshine and humidity in order to flourish. They can do just fine in a pot or planter. Just think if you had your own fresh pineapple growing in your home you could whip up a wonderful fresh pineapple smoothie to enjoy!

- **Dwarf Pomegranate Tree**—People will be sure to notice your amazing pomegranate tree; this is a tree that your neighbors probably do not own. The pomegranate tree will produce lovely flowers at first and then will come the miniature pomegranates. You will need to locate it in a sunny place in your home, and then it should do well and thrive. It will only grow to be about three feet tall.

- **Olive Tree**—You have most likely never thought about growing your own olive tree until now. An olive tree will be very happy in your home as long as it gets plenty of sunlight. What a great treat to serve your guests fresh olives. You will need to do a bit of pruning as olive trees can get a bit out of control, they prefer a drier climate and don't require daily watering.

- **Meyer Lemon Tree**—The Meyer lemon tree will take one to two years before it will begin to produce fruit. But it is very easy to grow indoors. The lemons you will get will taste far better than any lemon you buy at a store. Most of its lemons will be produced in the spring and summer. It will flower all year round leaving a lovely fragrance.

- **Miniature Orange Tree**—This is called a miniature orange tree but the fruit that it bares is more like a cross between kumquats and tangerines; however, indoor gardeners say it is one of the easiest things to grow. It smells wonderful when it flowers and it will generally produce the most fruit in the winter.

- **Dwarf Banana Tree**—The dwarf banana tree will grow to be about six feet tall, compared to the full-size that is about twice that. The bananas are smaller, they will measure around four or five inches each, but they taste just as good. The dwarf banana tree will start producing fruit for you in about one or two years opposed to three to five years with the full-size trees. This tree will be happy as long as it is getting enough sunlight. You could grab a couple of bananas of your dwarf banana tree to make a special treat like a yummy banana split!

Chapter 3 – Non-Tree Tropical Fruit

Perhaps growing fruit trees is not quite what you had in mind. Well there is no need to worry because there is a fruit that you can grow in planters or containers that will produce fruit for you just fine.

- **Passion Fruit—** Passion fruit actually grow on a vine and will produce amazing and lovely flowers as well as tasty fruit. The passion fruit flowers have a wonderful aroma that will make your home smell nice. The vine has large lush leaves that are a nice deep green that will be admired by your guests. You will need some kind of trellis or support for the vine to crawl around; you should cut it back as it could get out of control.

- **Melons**—Many people do not know that you can grow melons indoors, because of their sheer size, but there are several varieties of melons that you can grow indoors. The best of these varieties include Sugar baby, watermelon, Jenny Lind, watermelon golden midget, and Emerald gems. The key to success in growing melons indoors is to grow them vertically instead of horizontally.

When you are setting up to grow melons you will need a container for the plant and then you will need trellises for the melon plant to grow up and around. This could create a lovely backdrop in your sun-room. Make sure the spot where you are planning to grow your melons gets plenty of sunlight throughout the day.

- **Tomato**—One of the forgotten fruits is the tomato, but these you can also grow inside. You can start it from a seedling from a nursery or seeds. Get a pot, soil, and some plant stakes to help your tomato plant grow. Make sure that your tomato plant has access to sun and you will have tomatoes all year round.

During the winter months give your plant a quarter turn so that all sides are getting sun exposure. Some of the best varieties of tomatoes are Toy Boy, Patio, Pixie, Small Fry and Tiny Tim. These will make great indoor plants.

Strawberry—It can be easier to grow strawberries inside or in a pot for a few good reasons than growing them outside in your garden. When you grow strawberries in a garden they can take over your entire plot. It is hard to control their space when they are growing. Then there is pests that will steal your berries before you get a chance to enjoy them.

There are two popular ways to grow strawberries indoors. There is hanging a pot that you can use to grow strawberries. They work very well inside and out. Just try not to overfill the pots because then you could end up with mold issues.

You need to hand the pots in an area where they will be exposed to at least six hours a day of sunlight or the strawberries won't grow. You can also go with traditional style planting pots and plant your strawberries in them. Do not put too many plants in one pot. One of the best varieties of strawberries to grow indoors is the Alpine variety as they will tend to clump rather than spread out on the vine.

- **Pineapple**—Pineapples actually grow on a bush even though I mentioned it in the dwarf tree section, it really isn't a tree. It can reach up to six feet tall. So if you decide to grow pineapple plants be ready for tall plants. Keep it in a smaller container and trim it regularly this will keep it shorter.

Pineapple plants love lots of sun and they need to be watered regularly, but you can't make their soil too wet. A pineapple plant cannot tolerate frost. So if you take it outside make sure to bring it back inside before frost hits.

There are many different fruits that you can grow without a tree in your home, you can use alternative methods of raising your fruits, and you will soon find that you can grow a nice variety of exotic fruits in your home.

You will just love having all the lovely varieties of exotic fruit to choose from when you begin to grow them in your home. Fruits especially the exotic fruits in the supermarkets are so expensive most of the time, the average families cannot afford to buy them. Now when you start growing your own exotic fruits you will be able to offer your family great fresh organic exotic fruits that you know have not been exposed to any kind of sprays or chemicals.

They will also save you a lot of money compared to going to the supermarket and purchasing them there. If you grow your own exotic fruit you will be able to expand your family's intake of exotic fruits. It is highly likely that you do not buy a lot of exotic fruit like many people due to the high costs. But you will wipe that problem off the table once you begin to grow your own exotic fruits, and in a year or so they will begin to bare yummy sweet healthy chemical-free fruit for you and your family to enjoy for many years to come.

Chapter 4 – Tips & Tricks to Keep Your Fruit Healthy

Now you have a pretty good idea of the kinds of exotic fruits that you are interested in growing in your home. Starting this new way of providing yourself and family with fresh exotic fruits you should know that there are several important things that you will want to be aware of in order to be successful in growing your fruits. This way you will not be discouraged or disappointed if trouble occurs— instead you will know what to do. The following are some tricks and tips to help you get started with becoming a successful grower of exotic fruits.

- **Producing Fruit**—When you first start planting your fruit plants do not expect to get fruit within the first couple of months.

Many fruit plants and trees could take a year or two before they will produce fruit or longer. The full-size banana tree can take

up to five years before it will bare fruit. It is a good idea to pay attention to the time frame you are looking at for each fruit tree or plant.

You can always ask a local nursery if you are unsure about growing a certain tree or plant for some good advice.

- **Light**—This is a big problem that growers face with indoor plants, when they do not expose their plants to enough light. Many fruit trees and plants will need six to eight hours a day of direct sunlight so they are able to produce fruit. If your plants are setup in an actual sun-room you should be fine. But even so you should still keep an eye on them to make sure that they are not showing any signs of lack of sunshine such as if they start to whither. When the warm summer weather is here you should take your plants outdoors. During the summer months let them stay outside.

- **Pollination**—Many plants and trees you are going to grow will need to be pollinated by bees, which is another good reason to take your plants outside during the summer. This is going to help ensure that your plants will produce fruit. If you are unable to put your plants outside you can do the work of the bees yourself—you will need to do a bit of research to hand pollinate. Learn about the male and female parts of the tree or plant.

The process is basically the same where you take a ball of cotton, a Q-tip and gather pollen from the male flower. Once you have the pollen from the male flower, take that pollen and brush it gently onto the inside of the female flower of your plant. You will have to do the research to learn how to identify the differences between the male and female flowers on each individual plant, and you can also learn different ways to pollinate.

- **Soil**—Most plants and trees prefer a moist soil, but not overly wet or too damp, so make sure you are checking the soil often and keep it damp but not soaking wet. Make sure that your pot has proper drainage to keep it clear of excess water.

You should choose a soil that is rich in nutrients and you should consider using plant fertilizers specific for your type of plant or tree. There are specific fertilizers for citrus fruit trees, berries, melons, etc. So think about adding some of these as you care for your tree or plant. You will be given directions on the fertilizer when you should be giving your tree or plant some of it.

- **Pests & Insects**—Plants and trees can become infected with pests and insects. You will need to keep an eye out for this and be ready to treat your plants and trees right away.

An easy way to solve this is to wash the leaves and stems of your tree or plant with water. Using a spray bottle spray down your plant or tree.

- **Repotting**—Most of the trees and plants that you grow are going to need to be repotted at least once, some will need more than that. When you first purchase them you can keep them in the original container or transfer them into a similar size container.

You need to research to find out what the potential size of the plant or tree can be that you are planning on growing. They need to start in a small pot and work their way up to a bigger pot when they are ready to expand their root system.

- **Humidity**—Humidity in your home for the most part is fine for the majority of plants that we have looked at in this book.

There are a select few that use a small humidity boost in order to maintain their best productivity (it has been mentioned for the ones that need it).

If you decide to add a bit of humidity to your sun-room, choose something small and inexpensive that will mist your plants with just enough humidity that it will feel like Florida on a hot day in summer. It will most likely be in the winter months that your plants will need a humidity boost when things are cooler and drier.

- **Temperature**—This is another one of the important factors to pay attention with on individual plants or trees. Some plants can handle temperature fluctuations better than others. There are several options if you are struggling to try and keep your sun-room warm enough for your plants.

You can simply turn up the heat, but this can get expensive. You can buy a small space heater to install in your sun-room. You won't have to run extra heat except on really cold days.

- **Finding Indoor Dwarf Varieties**—You will find that it is not always easy to find plants and trees you are looking for, but if you go to online nurseries you can easily find the plants and trees you are searching for. You won't have to settle for something you don't really want, pay a bit more and get what you really want. There has been considerable improvement with online nurseries, they are doing a great job in getting your plants delivered to you just like you would get them if you went and picked them up at the nursery yourself. Often if you are not 100% pleased with the plant or tree you receive you will get your money-back or will get another plant or product for free. You may even be able to talk to your local nursery about putting in a special order for you.

- **Finding the Right Pots**—It can be tricky at times growing exotic fruits indoors with just any old pot. So it might be well worth your while to use a special kind of pot or trellis that was designed with your plant in mind.

You might be able to get what you are looking for by asking the local nursery to order the special items you request, local nurseries need loyal customers. If they are not willing to work with you then you still have online shopping. You will be able to find pretty much anything that you will need online. You may have to pay more to have the items shipped to you but in the end it will be worth it when you start to see the wonderful exotic fruits appearing on your trees and plants!

Conclusion

I hope that you will not feel intimidated about growing fruit trees and plants in your home. You have some great knowledge now on how you can do this in an effective manner that will suit your lifestyle. You certainly have a good assortment of fruits to choose from offered in this book. Remember if you do not have the space to grow a full-size tropical tree no worries you have many varieties of dwarf fruit trees to choose from that will take up little room in your home.

Make growing your own exotic fruits a family project get your kids involved in growing their own healthy snacks. Perhaps each family member could have a special tree or plant to their choice to call their own. Then watch their eyes light up when they see their own special tree or plant giving fruit for the first time!

Not only do you have an assortment of fruit trees to choose from but also fruit plants as well. You will not go wrong in growing your own fresh fruit supply for you and your family. Think how wonderful it is going to feel when you can save money and not rely on the local supermarket to supply you with your exotic fruits. You will also gain much comfort in knowing that your homegrown fruits are chemical-free! I wish you the best success in getting your green thumb greener by starting to grow your own exotic fruits at home!

Made in the USA
Las Vegas, NV
21 August 2021